Jesus
Gathering His Disciples

Matthew 4:18-23, 9:9-13, 10:2-42, 19:27-30
Mark 1:16-20, 2:14-20
Luke 5:2-11
John 1:43-51, 15:13-17

by

Rebecca Daniel

illustrated by
Nancee McClure

A Christian Education Activity Book

Cover by Nancee McClure
Copyright © Good Apple, Inc., 1984

ISBN No. 0-86653-224-2
Printing No. 98765

Shining Star Publications
A Division of Good Apple, Inc.
Box 299
Carthage, IL 62321-0299

NOTE: The activities in this book were written using the King James Version of the Bible, so always use this version to solve the puzzles.

The purchase of this book entitles the buyer to duplicate the activity pages as needed for use by students in the buyer's classroom. Permission for any other use must be granted by Shining Star Publications.

All rights reserved. Printed in the United States of America by Versa Press, Inc., East Peoria, IL.

INTRODUCTION

Jesus had much work to be done, so He gathered His twelve disciples to help Him and pass on His teachings. The adventure began one day while Jesus was walking by the Sea of Galilee. He saw two brothers casting a net into the sea, for these men were fishermen. They were called Simon Peter and Andrew. Jesus said to them, "Follow me, and I will make you fishers of men." They left their nets and followed Him.

Later, Jesus saw two other brothers, James and John, in a ship with Zebedee, their father. The fishermen were mending their nets. Jesus called to them to follow Him. "And they immediately left the ship and their father, and followed him."

Jesus' fame spread throughout all Syria because He healed many sick people. At a banquet, a tax collector named Matthew was called by Jesus. "And he arose, and followed him."

"The day following Jesus would go forth into Galilee, and findeth Philip, and saith unto him, Follow me." Then Philip went to get his friend named Nathanael. "Philip findeth Nathanael, and saith unto him, We have found him, of who Moses in the law, and the prophets, did write, Jesus of Nazareth, the son of Joseph." But Nathanael was full of doubt. He went to meet Jesus. When Jesus saw Nathanael, He said, "Before that Philip called thee, when thou was under the fig tree, I saw thee." Then Nathanael knew that Jesus was the long-awaited Savior.

Jesus chose five other men to be His disciples: Thomas, Thaddeus, James, Simon and Judas. Jesus taught His disciples how to heal the sick, cleanse the lepers, raise the dead and cast out devils.

He gave them wonderful words of wisdom. He told them to preach saying, "The kingdom of heaven is at hand." He said they should not worry about what to say to people, "for it shall be given you in the same hour what ye shall speak. For it is not ye that speak, but the Spirit of your Father."

Jesus taught people using parables and would explain the meaning of these parables to His disciples. "But many that are first shall be last; and the last shall be first." Jesus told the disciples that they were His friends. "I have called you friends; for all things that I have heard of my Father I have made known unto you." And He gave the disciples a new commandment: "Love one another, as I have loved you."

Shining Star Publication, Copyright © 1984, A division of Good Apple, Inc.

CALLING OF PETER AND ANDREW

Matthew 4:18-20; Mark 1:16-18; Luke 5:2-9

Use the number code to solve this puzzle.
A=1, B=2, C=3, D=4, E=5, F=6, G=7, H=8, I=9,
J=10, K=11, L=12, M=13, N=14, O=15, P=16,
Q=17, R=18, S=19, T=20, U=21, V=22, W=23,
X=24, Y=25, Z=26

10,5,19,21,19   14,5,5,4,5,4   8,5,12,16   23,8,5,14   8,5
_____   _____   _____   _____   __

23,5,14,20   20,15   16,18,5,1,3,8   9,14   7,1,12,9,12,5,5.
_____   __   _____   __   _____

1,19   8,5   23,1,12,11,5,4   2,25   20,8,5   19,5,1   15,6
__   __   _____   __   ___   ___   __

7,1,12,9,12,5,5,   8,5   19,1,23   20,23,15
_____   __   ___   ___

6,9,19,8,5,18,13,5,14.   20,8,5,25   23,5,18,5
_____   ____   ____

2,18,15,20,8,5,18,19   14,1,13,5,4   19,9,13,15,14
_____   _____   _____

16,5,20,5,18   1,14,4   1,14,4,18,5,23.   10,5,19,21,19
_____   ___   _____   _____

3,1,12,12,5,4   20,15   20,8,5,13   1,14,4   20,8,5,25
_____   __   _____   ___   ____

12,5,6,20   20,8,5,9,18   6,9,19,8,9,14,7   14,5,20,19   1,14,4
____   ____   _____   ____   ___

6,15,12,12,15,23,5,4   10,5,19,21,19.
_____   _____

Name_____

Decode the secret message. Some of the letters have been replaced with numbers. You must decide which letters stand for which numbers.

A = __   E = __   F = __   H = __   I = __   L = __   M = __   O = __

SECRET MESSAGE: "__ __ __ __ __ __   __ __,
__ __ __   __   __ __ __ __   __ __ __ __   __ __ __
__ __ __ __ __ __ __   __ __   __ __ __."

"4,2,5,5,2,W   1,6   8,N,D   7   W,7,5,5

1,8,K,6   Y,2,U   4,7,S,3,6,R,S   2,4

1,6,N."

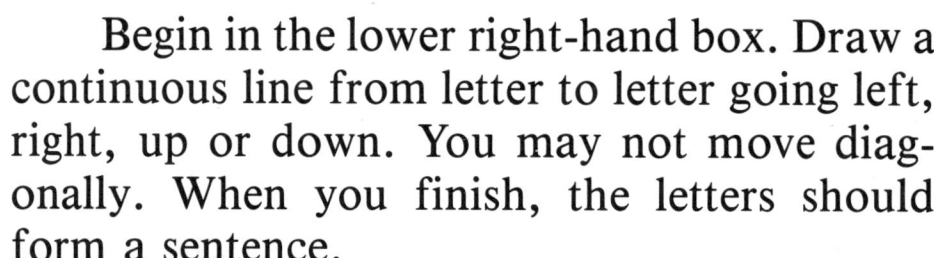

Begin in the lower right-hand box. Draw a continuous line from letter to letter going left, right, up or down. You may not move diagonally. When you finish, the letters should form a sentence.

SECRET MESSAGE: __ __ __ __
__ __ __ __ __ __ __ __ __   __ __ __ .

D	E	W	O
H	I	M	L
Y	F	O	L
E	H	T	*

Name_____

CALLING OF JAMES AND JOHN

Matthew 4:21-23; Mark 1:19,20; Luke 5:10,11

To discover the secret message, write the letter of the alphabet that comes before each letter found below. There is no letter before the letter A. In this code, A = Z.

KFTVT TBX UXP PUIFS CSPUIFST,
JESUS SAW TWO OTHER BROTHERS,

KBNFT BOE KPIO, JO B TIJQ
JAMES AND JOHN, IN A SHIP

XJUI AFCFEFF, UIFJS GBUIFS.
WITH ZEBEDEE, THEIR FATHER.

XIFO KFTVT DBMMFE UIFN, UIFZ
WHEN JESUS CALLED THEM, THEY

MFGU UIF TIJQ BOE UIFJS
LEFT THE SHIP AND THEIR

GBUIFS BOE GPMMPXFE IJN.
FATHER AND FOLLOWED HIM.

Name_____

Unscramble the words below and write the secret message.

NAD   SUJES   NEWT   TBAOU   LAL

____   _____   _____   _____   ___

ELLGAIE   GIAETCHN,   GIAEPRCHN

_____   _____   _____

ETH   EOGSPL   NAD   NIAEHLG

___   _____   ___   _____

SSEISCKN.

_____

Can you spell 12 words mentioned in the Scriptures using only the letters in the box found below?

T	A	L
G	P	E
R	N	C
H	I	O

_____   _____

_____   _____

_____   _____

_____   _____

_____   _____

_____   _____

Name_____

Shining Star Publication, Copyright © 1984, A division of Good Apple, Inc.

CALLING OF MATTHEW
Matthew 9:9-13; Mark 2:14-20

Cross out one letter in each word below to spell new words and discover the answer to this puzzle. Then write your own message and put one extra letter in each word. Ask a friend to solve your puzzle.

TONE   DAYS   JESUSS   SLAW
____   ____   _____   ____

MATTHEEW,   AM   STAX
_____   __   ____

COLLECTORS.   JESUSE   SLAID,
_____   _____   _____

"FOLLOWE   MEN,   MATTHEWS."
_____   ___   _____

MATTHEWS   SLEFT   WHEAT   SHE
_____   _____   _____   ___

WAST   DOINGS   LAND   BECAMEL
____   _____   ____   _____

TONE   OFF   JESUS'S   DISCIPLESS.
____   ___   _____   _____

Name_____

All the vowels in the message below are incorrect. Replace the incorrect vowels with the correct vowels, and you will discover the secret message.

"A EM NET CAMI TE CELL
___ ___ ___ ____ __ ____

THA REGHTIUES, BAT SENNURS
___ _____ ___ _____

TA RAPINTENCA."
__ _____

The designs below are actually words. Find the hidden letters in each design to form words which will solve this puzzle.

ANSWER: ___ ___ ___ _____ ____ ___ ?

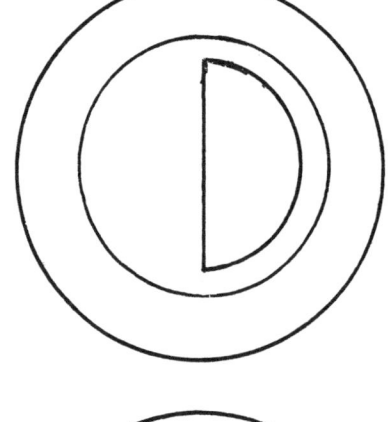
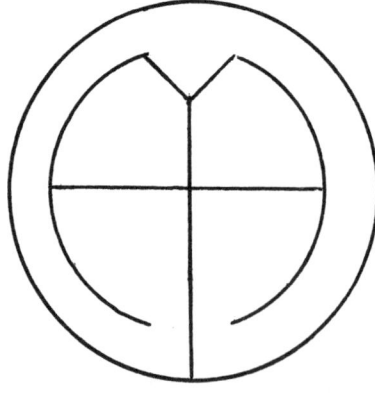
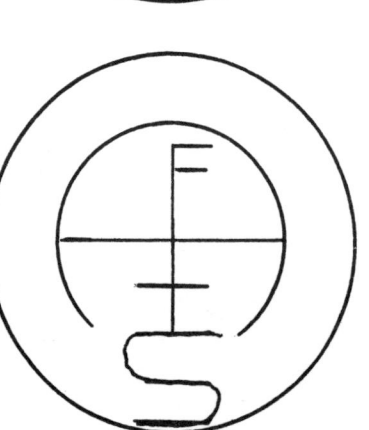

Name_____

CALLING OF PHILIP

John 1:43,44

Find the shortest path through the maze. Color the path. To discover the message, write the letters in the order they are found.

SECRET MESSAGE: _ _ _ _ _ _

_ _ _ _ _   _ _ _ _ _ _ .

Name_____

What word found in the Scriptures can you put in the middle that makes three-letter words of the letters going down?

o	p	i	a	s	o	p	i	e
f	p	l	l	w	l	n	n	g

To discover the secret message, follow the lines and write the letters in the order they are found.

SECRET MESSAGE: _ _ _ _ _ _ _

_ _ _ _ _ _ _ _ _ _ _ _ ,

_ _ _ _ _ _ _ _

_ _ _ _ _ _ _ _ _ _ _ .

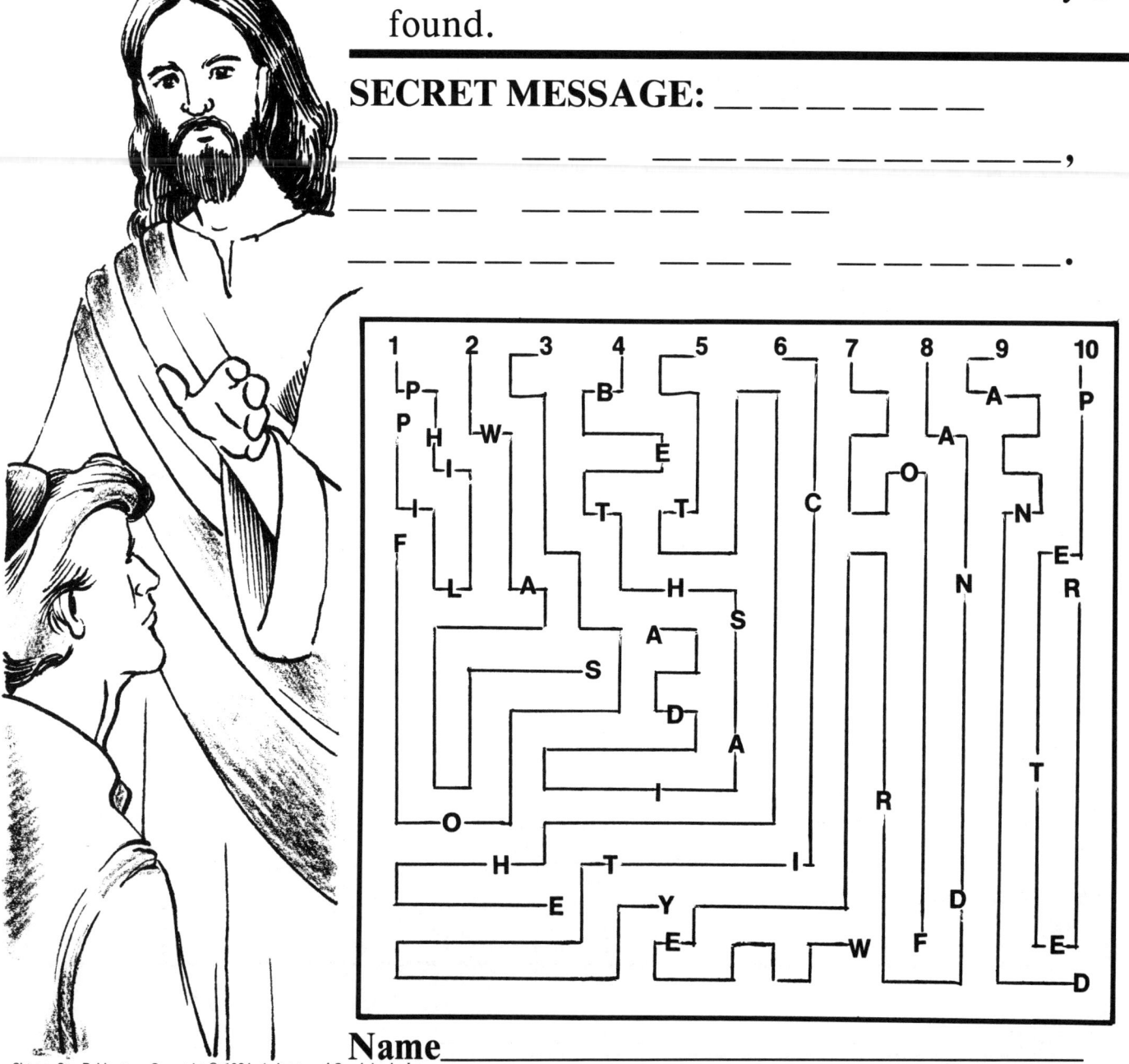

Name _____

CALLING OF NATHANAEL
John 1:45-51

To discover the secret message, follow the directions carefully.

MTOLOM   FIUND   NEHTENEAL   END
____   ____   _____   ___

SEOD   HI   TOP,   "WA   TEVA   FIUND
____   __   ___   __   ____   ____

TOP,   JASUS   IF   NEZERAHT,   HTA
___   _____   __   _____   ___

SIN   IF   JISAMT.   TA   OS   HTA   INA
___   __   _____   __   __   ___   ___

PISAS   END   HTA   MRIMTAHS
_____   ___   ___   _____

WRIHA   EBIUH."
_____   _____

Change all the A's to E's.
Change all the E's to A's.
Change all the T's to H's.
Change all the H's to T's.
Change all the P's to M's.
Change all the M's to P's.
Change all the O's to I's.
Change all the I's to O's.
The other letters are correct.

Name_____

Shining Star Publication, Copyright © 1984, A division of Good Apple, Inc.

11

Below are three words from the Scriptures. They have been scrambled together. Can you unscramble these three words?

ANSWER: "_ ."

NETTHEDINNFILLPAPHIHAA

To discover the secret message, write every other letter moving clockwise around the circle. You must decide where to begin.

SECRET MESSAGE: "Philip saith _ _ _ _ _ _ _ _, _ _ _ _ _ _ _ _ _ _."

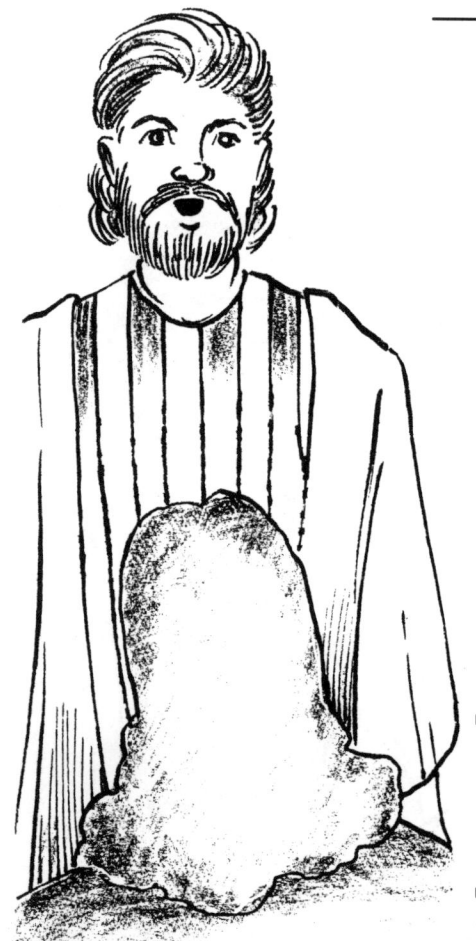

Make up your own circle puzzle using the Scriptures.

Name_____

THE APOSTLES ARE ALL NAMED

Matthew 10:2-5

In each row of jumbled letters found below is a hidden word. To discover the secret message, circle the hidden words and write them in the order they are found on the blanks below.

SECRET MESSAGE: _____ _____ _____ ____ _____ : _____, _____, _____, ____, _____, _____, _____, _____, _____, _____, _____, _____ ___ _____.

```
Y I E I R M N D T H E S E K T E O R O M
K D I T T W E L V E B K E I D M O N D D
J E K I J E S U S K D O S J F I R K E M
S E N T I D K T Y E O U D M L N T I F I
Y I M O N F O F F O R T H H N T M K E E
M I E U K F K R P E T E R N D H A J E E
K D I E A N D R E W I W I E K E E K M O
I E J K M E J A M E S I E K D N E I E M
Y I E M D N J O H N I E K D M N E I K D
P H I L I P E J B I R K D F L A W E E R
I E K D N M O I D J N A T H A N A E L L
I E M D N T H O M A S K E I D M I K D I
K D U M I N A J J E A J A M E S I D K E
K E I D H M E M A T T H E W I D K E D E
K E I T J E H T H A D D E U S K E K D M
K D I E M D I E N S I M O N E I D K E N
L J P A S E T A N D A S I K A Z B A E N
J D I M O N D K J I E J D M O J U D A S
```

Name _____

Find the names of the twelve disciples hidden in the letter maze. They may read across, down, or diagonally. Be very careful to find the correct spelling of each name.

A CHALLENGE: Can you find another name for Nathanael hidden in the puzzle?

```
N J M A T T H A W E X
P A J E M E J O N J Y
E M T H O M A S J O B
T E P H I L I P O T A
E S J A A R J O N H R
S S I M O N E P H A T
M J E M S J A E T D H
A S A J O O U E E D O
T I N M N H M D L E L
T M D H E N J A A U O
H A R J O S J O H S M
E N E P E T E R J S E
W J W O H N J A M E W
```

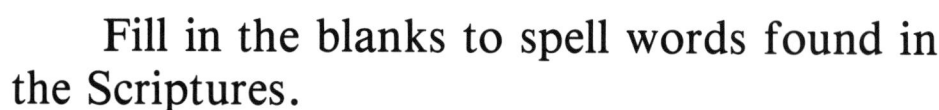

Fill in the blanks to spell words found in the Scriptures.

__ o	__ __ __ o
__ o	__ __ __ o
o __	__ o __ __
__ o __	__ __ o __ __
__ o __	__ o __
__ o __	__ __ o __ __ __
__ __ o	__ __ o __ __ __

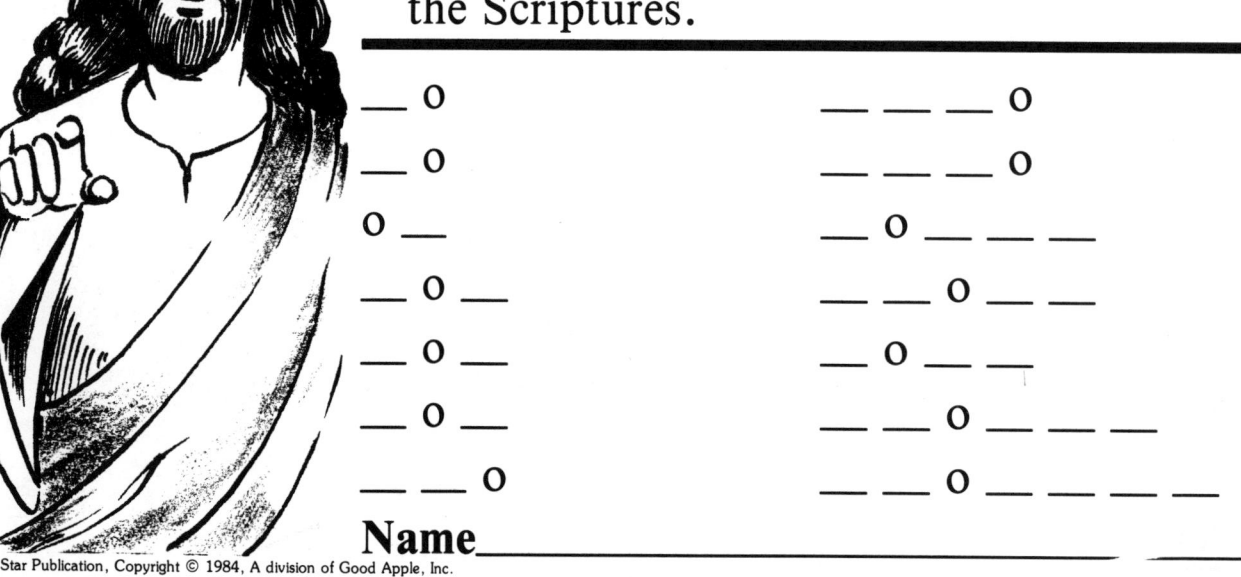

Name_____

GO TO THE LOST SHEEP

Matthew 10:6-11

To discover the secret message, follow the directions carefully.

SECRET MESSAGE: "___ ___ ___

___ ___ ___ ___ ___ ___ ___   ___ ___

___ ___ ___ ___ ___ ___   ___ ___   ___ ___

___ ___ ___ ___."

1. M A T T H E W S I X T H E O X
2. J A M E S K I N G D O M T E N
3. Z F I F T Y S I M O N O F Z Z
4. Z H E A V E N P E T E R A N T
5. A N D R E W Z I S S E V E N Z
6. C O W P H I L I P A T B L U E
7. T H A D D E U S R E D H A N D

Cross out the name of a disciple in each line.
Cross out the number in lines 1,2,3 and 5.
Cross out the color word in lines 6 and 7.
Cross out the animal in lines 1,4 and 6.
Cross out all the Z's in the puzzle.

Name_____

Begin in the upper left-hand corner and end in the lower right-hand corner. Find a path through the letters that spells a message. You must move across or down. You may not move diagonally.

SECRET MESSAGE: "Provide neither

_ _ _ _ _, _ _ _ _ _ _ _ _,
_ _ _ _ _ _ _ _...."

```
G   O   L   G   G   O   L   G   G   O
O   L   D   O   L   O   D   O   O   L
L   D   N   O   R   L   N   L   D   D
D   N   O   R   S   D   O   D   D   N
N   O   O   S   O   N   N   R   N   O
O   S   I   I   L   V   E   S   O   R
R   S   I   L   V   O   R   I   R   S
S   I   L   E   R   N   N   L   S   I
E   L   V   E   N   O   O   V   I   L
L   V   E   R   O   R   B   R   A   V
V   E   R   N   O   R   B   A   S   S
```

Circle the first letter and then circle every third letter to discover the answer to this puzzle.

ANSWER: "_ _ _ _ _ _ _ _
_ _ _ _, _ _ _ _ _ _ _ _ _ _
_ _ _ _ _ _ _, _ _ _ _ _ _ _ _
_ _ _ _ _, _ _ _ _ _ _ _
_ _ _ _ _ _ _...."

```
H W Q E R T A H N L U Y T H G H O I E T Y S T Y I U H C K M K P
O C H G L N B E M C A Y T N W Q S R T E Y U T R E H W Q E O P L
R W E Y T P M N E I U R W Q S Y T R P O A Q E I N B S E R E S X
T R E H Q W E G B D W A E R S A U I D V B C W E A T Y S Q E T U
I O P K U R E T Y T D R W E B N V O K I P O L W Q S U Y
```

Name_____

IN THE MIDST OF WOLVES

Matthew 10:12-16

Add the correct vowel in each space to spell words and discover the secret message. Let the Scriptures help you. Then write your own message and leave out the vowels. See if a friend can decode your message.

"_ND WH_S__V_R SH_LL N_T

___ _____ _____ ___

R_C__V_ Y__, N_R H__R

_____ ___ ___ ____

Y__R W_RDS, WH_N Y_

____ _____ ____ ___

D_P_RT __T _F TH_T

_____ ___ __ ____

H__S_ _R C_TY, SH_K_ _FF

_____ __ ____ _____ ___

TH_ D_ST _F Y__R F__T."

___ ____ __ ____ ____

Name_____

Let the Scriptures help you solve this puzzle.

"(2 down), I send you (4 across) as sheep in the midst (6 down) (7 across): be ye (1 down) wise as (8 across), and (3 across) as (5 across)."

Matthew 10:16

YOU WILL BE BROUGHT BEFORE GOVERNORS.

Three letters in this message have been replaced with the letter *X*. Can you decode this message by filling in the correct letters?

"AND IF XXE XXUSE BE
___ ___ ___ ___
WXRXXY, LEX YXUR PEACE
___ ___ ___ ___
CXME UPXN IX. . . ."
___ ___ ___

Name_____

FOR MY SAKE

Matthew 10:17-20

Color the T's after the sentence if the statement is true. Color the F's after the sentence if the statement is false. The T's and F's will make letters. Fill in the blanks with the appropriate letters to discover the secret word.

SECRET WORD:

$\overline{} \ \overline{} \ \overline{} \ \overline{} \ \overline{} \ \overline{}$
  1   2   3   4   5   6

1. Jesus said to beware of men.
   TTTTT
   TFFFF
   TTTTT
   FFFFT
   TTTTT

2. Jesus said men will praise the disciples.
   FFFFF
   FTTTF
   FFFFF
   FTTTT
   FTTTT

3. Jesus said the disciples would be brought before kings.
   FTTTF
   FFTFF
   FFTFF
   FFTFF
   FTTTF

4. Jesus told the disciples to think hard before they spoke.
   FFFFT
   FTTFT
   FFFTT
   FTTFT
   FTTTF

5. Jesus told the disciples that it is not they who would speak.
   FTTTF
   FFTFF
   FFTFF
   FFTFF
   FTTTF

6. Jesus said the Spirit of the Father would speak for the disciples.
   TTTTT
   FFTFF
   FFTFF
   FFTFF
   FFTFF

Name_____

Complete these word stars by spelling words found in the Scriptures. In each star, the words always have the same middle letter.

1.
2.
3.

Can you find an antonym in the Scriptures for each word listed below? Use the antonyms you find to complete the puzzle found below.

overlook _____   give _____
women _____   yes _____
retain _____   taken _____
after _____

Name_____

MORE VALUE THAN SPARROWS

Matthew 10:29-31

Can you read this rebus message? Let the Scriptures help you. Then write your own rebus message about this story.

Matthew 10:29,30

"R  2 sp + 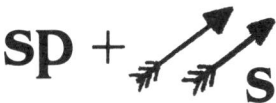 S + old 4 A farthing? & 1 of T +  shall  f + ⚾ − B on the ⛰ without U + R Father. But the V + 🍇 − B s of U + R  R all numbered."

Name_____

To discover the secret message, use the consonants listed below and complete the words. Cross out each letter when you have used it.

B D D F H H H M N R R R R S T Y

__E _AI__ O_ _OU_ _EA_ A_E _U__E_E_.

F N R T

_EA_ _O_.

B H L L M M N N P R R R R S S T V W Y Y

_OU A_E _O_E _A_UA__E __A_ _A__ __A__O__.

What word found in the Scriptures can you put in the middle that makes three-letter names of the letters going down?

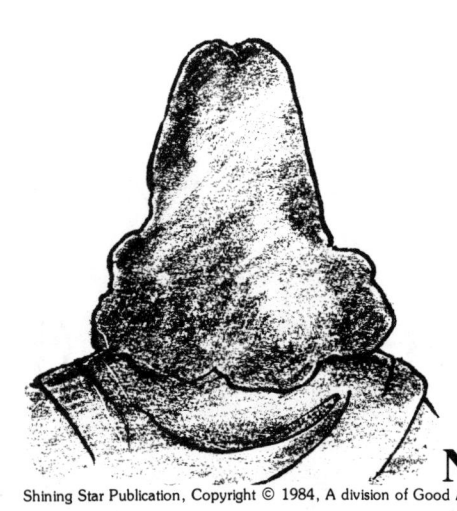

A	B	A	A	L	A	T	I
N	D	Y	E	E	T	D	A

Name_____

22

FOLLOWETH AFTER ME

Matthew 10:38-42

To discover the secret message, you will need your crayons. Color the spaces with one dot GREEN. Color the spaces with two dots PINK.

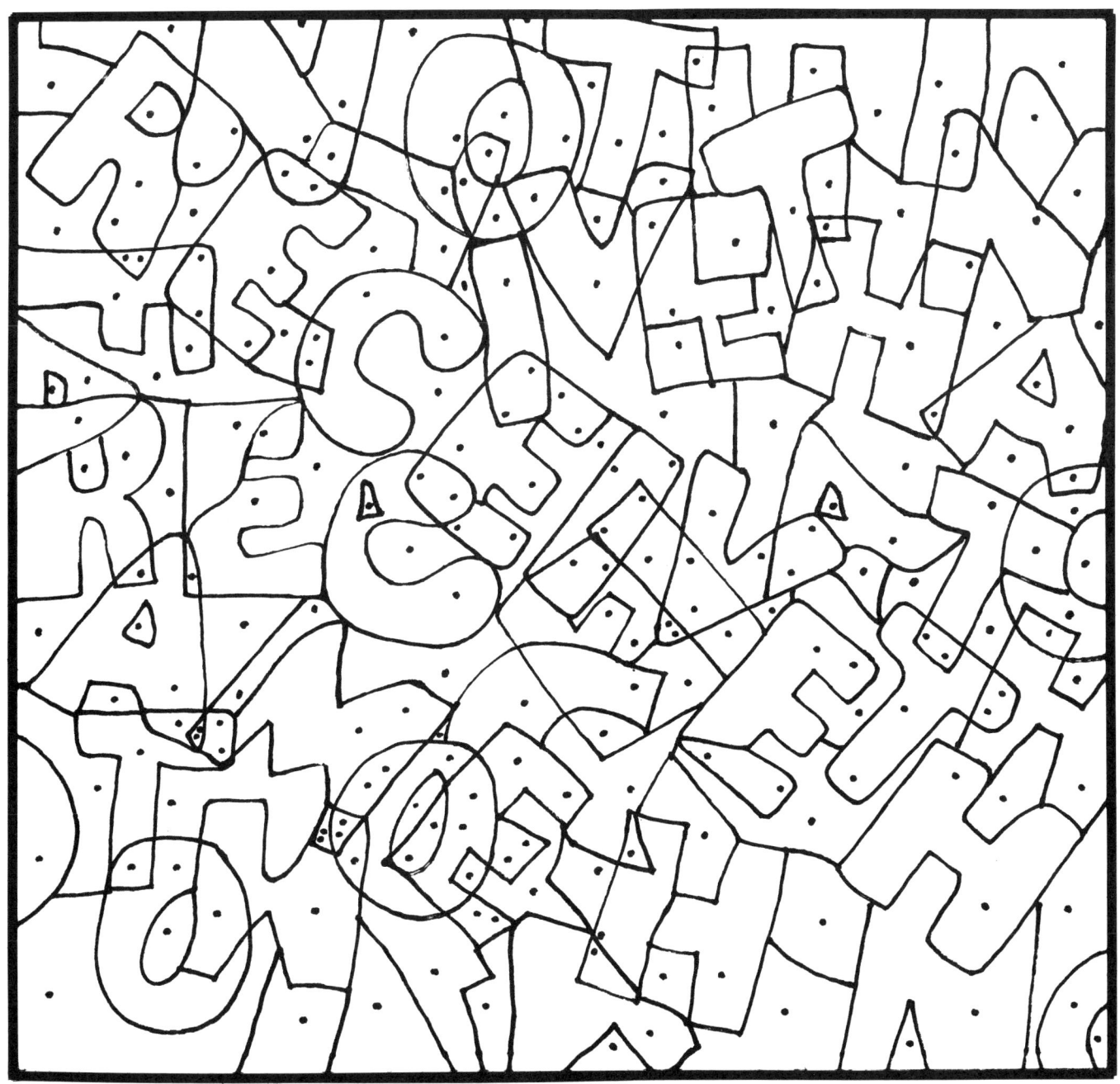

Name_____

Let the Scriptures help you solve this puzzle. Fill in the blanks with the correct words. Then place these words in the puzzle.

"__ __ that __ __ __ __ __ __ __ __ __ you receiveth __ __, and he that receiveth __ me."

Matthew 10:40

The puzzle below has two words scrambled together. Use the clues to discover both words.

S H E I C E P P P I D R L O T

Remove the one who speaks for another and you will be left with one who receives instructions from another.

The one who speaks for another is called a

__ __ __ __ __ __ __ __ __.

The one who receives instructions from another is called a

__ __ __ __ __ __ __ __ __.

Name_____

24

THE LAST SHALL BE FIRST

Matthew 19:27-30

To decode this message, use the code found below.

S	E	R
A	G	I
U	Y	L

N.	T.	O.
D.	F.	C.
H.	W.	M.

"... ___ ___ ___ ___,

___ ___ ___ ___

___ ___ ... ___

___ ___ ___ ___

___ ___ ___...."

Name_____

Finish these magic word squares by spelling words found in the Scriptures. The words must read down as well as across.

1.

E	V	E	N

2.

H	A	L	T

3.

T			
H			
O			
U			

4.

H	A	L	L

Make up your own magic word squares using words found in the Scriptures.

Name_____

I HAVE CHOSEN YOU
John 15:13-17

Complete each word by adding one letter. The words are all found in the Scriptures. Then read down to discover the secret message.

SECRET MESSAGE: "__ __   __ __ __   __ __   __ __ __ __ __ __ __...."

__ou
gr__ater
h__th
f__uit
lov__
__an
la__

__or
a__e
l__fe
do__th
__ot
shoul__
thing__

Name_____

Read each sentence. Decide if each statement was made by Jesus. If the statement was made by Jesus, circle the letter under the letter *T*. If the statement was not made by Jesus, circle the letter under the letter *F*. To discover the secret message, fill in the blanks with the appropriate letters.

SECRET MESSAGE: __ __
                     1   2

___ ___ ___ ___ ___ ___ ___   ___ ___ ___ ___
 3   4   5   6   7   8   9   10 11 12 13

		T	F			T	F
1. "I call you not servants."		N	E	9. "You should sing songs to me."		Q	R
2. "The servant knoweth not what his Lord doeth."		O	I	10. "A man will lay down his life for a friend."		L	B
3. "I have called you friends."		G	U	11. "I have made known unto you that which I have heard of my Father."		O	A
4. "Ye have chosen me."		A	R				
5. "I have chosen you."		E	I				
6. "I have ordained you."		A	O	12. "Ye shall ask of the Father in my name."		V	G
7. "You should go and bring forth fruit."		T	J	13. "I command that you love one another."		E	A
8. "You should fish with your nets."		R	E				

Begin in the box with the asterisk. Draw a continuous line from letter to letter going left, right, up or down. You may not move diagonally. When you finish, the letters should form a sentence.

ANSWER: "__ __ __ __ __ __ __ __ __ __ __ __ . . . ."

Name_____

I HAVE CHOSEN YOU

John 15:13-17

Can you spell 18 words that are found in John 15:13-17 using the letter maze below? Begin in any circle and move along circles that are connected by a line. List the words that you find.

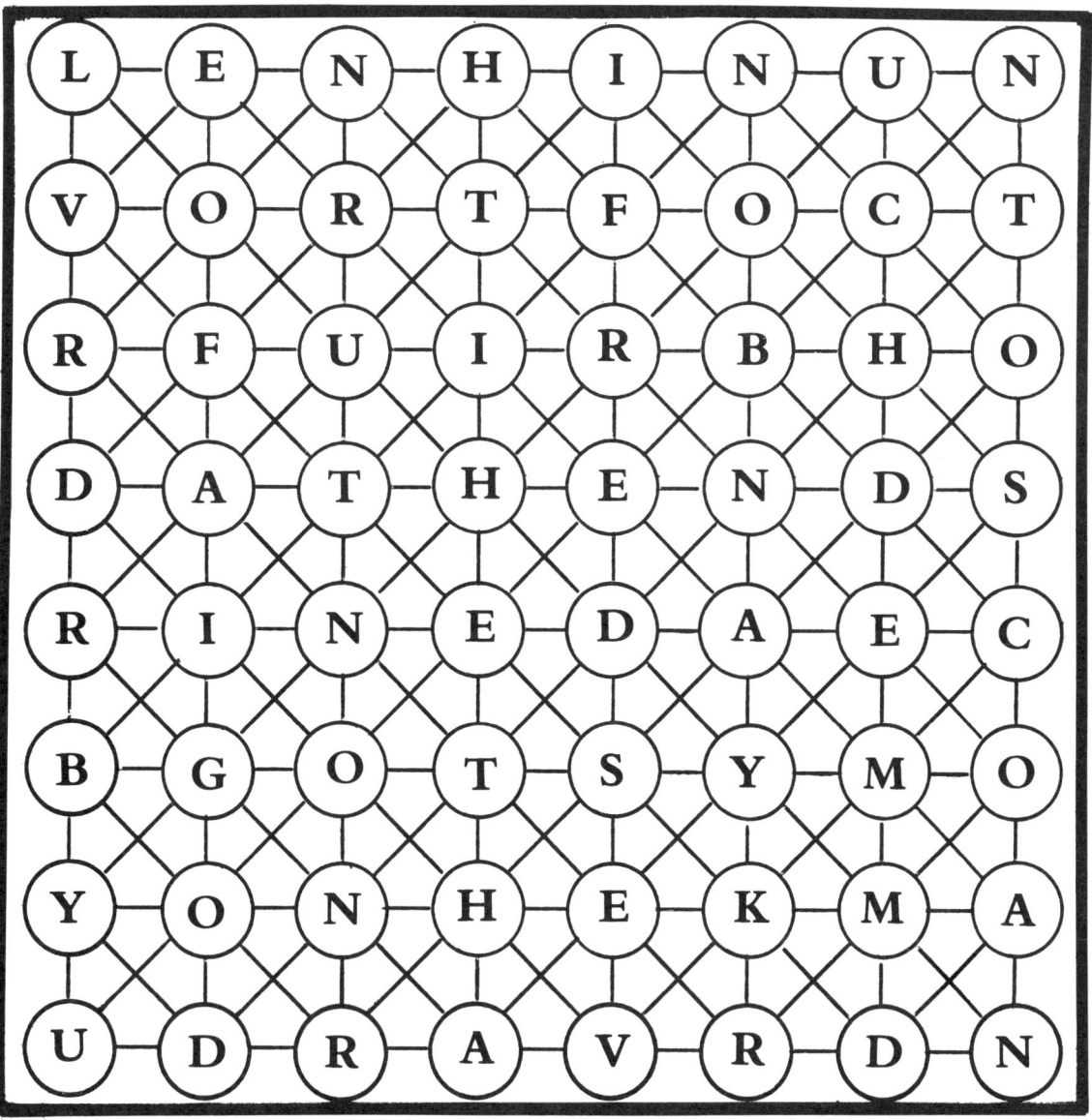

Name_____

PRE AND POST-TEST

Read the statements below. If the statement is true, color the appropriately numbered spaces ORANGE. If the statement is false, color the appropriately numbered spaces PURPLE.

1. Jesus chose twelve men to help Him.
2. Simon Peter and Andrew were the two sons of Zebedee.
3. Jesus told Simon Peter and Andrew He would make them fishers of men.
4. Thomas was a tax collector who followed Jesus.
5. Philip asked his friend Nathanael to come to see Jesus.
6. Nathanael was sometimes called Bartholomew.
7. Jesus went to a banquet at the home of Matthew.
8. Jesus said that the disciples were His friends.
9. Jesus taught the disciples how to heal sick people.
10. Jesus told the disciples what His parables meant.
11. Jesus gave the disciples ten new commandments.
12. Jesus told the disciples that the Father would speak through them.

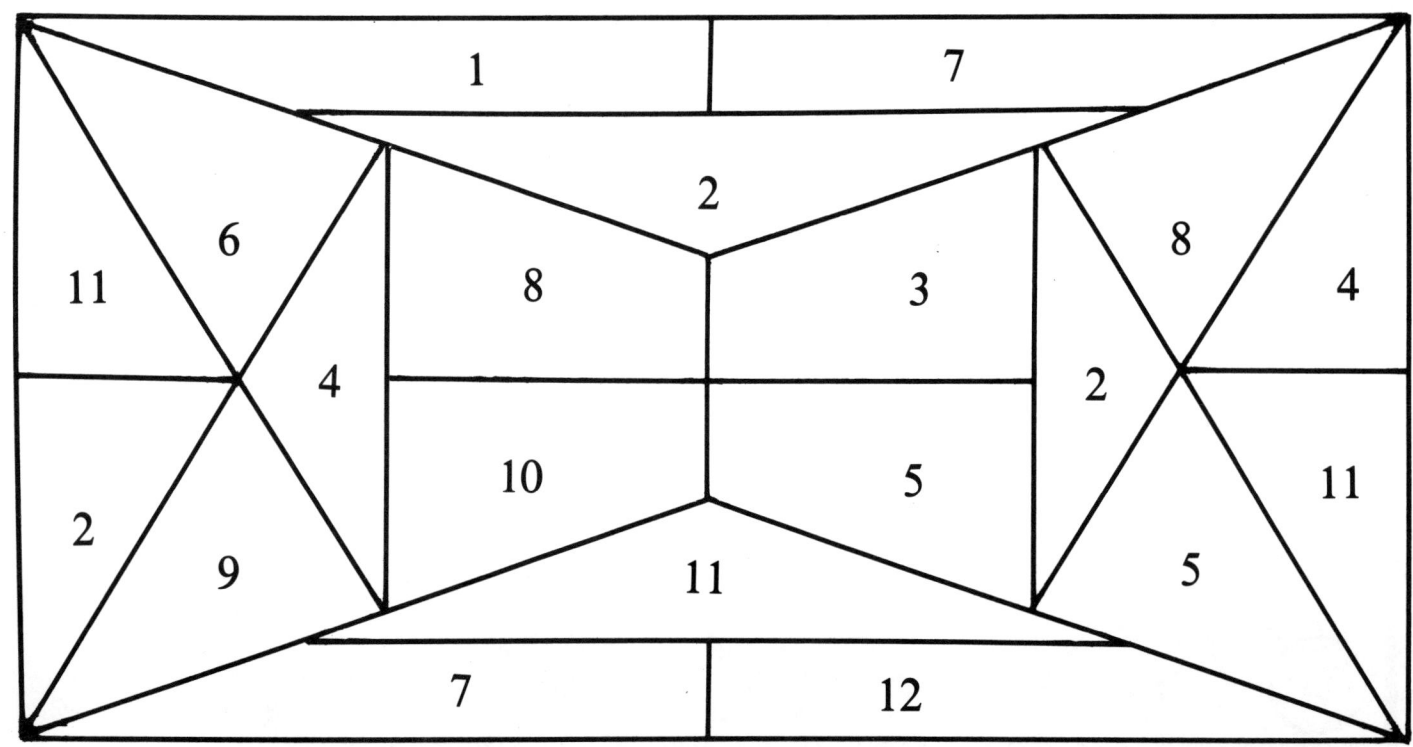

Name_____

ANSWER KEY

3. Jesus needed help when He went to preach in Galilee. As He walked by the Sea of Galilee, He saw two fishermen. They were brothers named Simon Peter and Andrew. Jesus called to them and they left their fishing nets and followed Jesus.

4. A = 8, E = 6, F = 4, H = 3, I = 7, L = 5, M = 1, O = 2
"Follow me, and I will make you fishers of men."
They followed Him.

5. Jesus saw two other brothers, James and John, in a ship with Zebedee, their father. When Jesus called them, they left the ship and their father and followed Him.

6. And Jesus went about all Galilee teaching, preaching the gospel and healing sickness.
teaching, preaching, healing, going, on, He, other, the, in, their, all, Galilee

7. One day Jesus saw Matthew, a tax collector. Jesus said, "Follow me, Matthew." Matthew left what he was doing and became one of Jesus' disciples.

8. "I am not come to call the righteous, but sinners to repentance."
WHY DO THY DISCIPLES FAST NOT?

9. JESUS FOUND PHILIP.

10. following
PHILIP WAS OF BETHSAIDA, THE CITY OF ANDREW AND PETER.

11. Philip found Nathanael and said to him, "We have found Him, Jesus of Nazareth, the son of Joseph. He is the one Moses and the Prophets wrote about."

12. "Philip findeth Nathanael."
"Philip saith unto him, come and see."

13. These twelve Jesus sent forth: Peter, Andrew, James, John, Philip, Nathanael, Thomas, James, Matthew, Thaddeus, Simon and Judas.

14.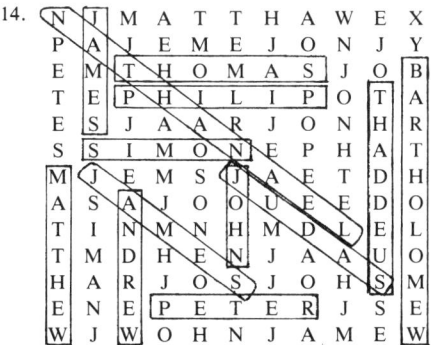

to, go, of, now, not, son, who, also, into, forth, whose, John, Thomas, brother

15. "The kingdom of heaven is at hand."

16. "Provide neither gold, nor silver, nor brass . . . ."

```
G O L G G G O L G G O
O L D O L O O D O O L
L D N O R L L N L L D
D N O R S D D O D D N
N O O S O N N R N N O
O S I L V E S O O R
R S I L V O R I R R S
S I L E R N N L S S I
E L V E N O O V I L L
L V E R O R R B R A V
V E R N O R B A S S S
```

"Heal the sick, cleanse the lepers, raise the dead, cast out devils . . . ."

17. "And whosoever shall not receive you, nor hear your words, when ye depart out of that house or city, shake off the dust of your feet . . . ."

18. Across:
3. harmless
4. forth
5. doves
7. wolves
8. serpents
Down:
1. therefore
2. behold
6. of
"And if the house be worthy, let your peace come upon it . . . ."

19. SPIRIT
1. T, 2. F, 3. T, 4. F, 5. T, 6. T

20. 1. deliver, against
2. for, you, how, not
3. scourge, brought, thought

Across:
4. beware
5. no
6. given
7. before
Down:
1. deliver
2. take
3. men

21. "Are not two sparrows sold for a farthing? and one of them shall not fall on the ground without your Father. But the very hairs of your head are all numbered."

22. The hairs of your head are numbered.
Fear not.
You are more valuable than many sparrows.
numbered

23. RECEIVETH ME

24. "He that receiveth you receiveth me, and he that receiveth me receiveth him that sent me."
Across:
3. receiveth
6. sent
7. me
Down:
1. he
2. him
3. receiveth
4. that
5. me
prophet, disciple

25. ". . . I say unto you, that ye which have followed me . . . shall sit in the throne of his glory . . . ."

26.
```
l a s t      h a l t
i    h      a    h
f    e      t    e
e v e n      h a v e
t h a t      h a l l
h    h      a    i
o    e      t    f
u p o n      h a v e
```

27. "Ye are my friends. . . ."

28. NO GREATER LOVE
1. T, 2. T, 3. T, 4. F, 5. T, 6. T, 7. T, 8. F, 9. F, 10. T, 11. T, 12. T, 13. T
"I have chosen you . . . ."

29. love, friends, Father, chosen, ordained, bring, forth, fruit, you, unto, ask, name, may, one, another, command, servant, heard, no, for

30. true: 1,3,5,6,7,8,9,10,12
false: 2,4,11

AWARD CERTIFICATE

This is to certify that

_____

has successfully completed a study of Jesus gathering
His disciples. The Scriptures covered
Matthew 4:18-23, 9:9-13, 10:2-42, 19:27-30;
Mark 1:16-20, 2:14-20; Luke 5:2-11;
John 1:43-51, 15:13-17.

_____
signature (teacher)

_____
signature (pastor)

_____
date

Shining Star Publication, Copyright © 1984, A division of Good Apple, Inc.